REFUSING TO GIVE UP IN PRAYER

Christopher Love

Importunity: Refusing to Give Up in Prayer

is a revised edition of

The Zealous Christian Holding Communion with God in Wrestling and Importunate Prayer

By Christopher Love (1618-1651)

Published by

CORNER PILLAR PRESS
Forest, VA
© 2016 Jennifer Adams
All Rights Reserved

Printed in the United States of America

ISBN: 978-0-9976251-0-3

cornerpillarpress@gmail.com
www.cornerpillarpress.com

Cover Design:
Mary Bethany Adams

Cover Layout:
Jonathan Harris

Front Cover Picture:
The Importunate Neighbor
by William Holman Hunt (1895)

PRAYER TRILOGY
by Corner Pillar Press

THE GOD WHO ANSWERS PRAYER: THE WORK OF THE
FATHER, SON, AND SPIRIT IN PRAYER
David Clarkson

THE RETURN OF PRAYERS: SOWING SEEDS OF PRAYER
AND WAITING ON GOD FOR A HARVEST OF ANSWERS
Thomas Goodwin

IMPORTUNITY: REFUSING TO GIVE UP IN PRAYER
Christopher Love

Other Works from CORNER PILLAR PRESS:

The Fountain of Life: A Display of Christ in His Essential and Mediatorial Glory, John Flavel
Preparation for Suffering, John Flavel

"Completer to a Contender for the Faith" Series:

A Basket of Summer Fruit, Susannah Spurgeon
Edited and annotated by Jennifer Adams
In Love with Christ: The Narrative of Sarah Edwards,
Edited and annotated by Jennifer Adams
Ann Judson: Missionary Wife, VOLUME I of
The Lives of the Three Mrs. Judsons, Arabella Stuart,
Revised, edited, and annotated by Jennifer Adams
Delighting in Her Heavenly Bridegroom:
The Memoirs of Harriet Newell, Teenage Missionary Wife,
Edited and annotated by Jennifer Adams
Following Her Beloved: The Memoirs of Henrietta Shuck,
Missionary Wife and Mother,
Compiled by Jeremiah Bell Jeter,
Edited and annotated by Jennifer Adams
With Cords of Love: The Memoirs of Elizabeth Dwight:
Missionary Wife and Mother,
Compiled by Harrison Dwight,
Edited and annotated by Jennifer Adams

Contents

Chapter 1

The Foundation of Answered Prayer
ॐ

*I say unto you, though he will not rise and give to him because he
is his friend, yet because of his importunity, he will give him as
much as he needs.*
Luke 11:8

MY Text is the conclusion of a familiar parable used by Christ
whereby he instructed his disciples on the doctrine and practice of
prayer. The occasion upon which Christ addressed this subject is
found in Luke 11:1 where one of his disciples said, "Lord, teach us
to pray as John also taught his disciples." Whether it was one of the
twelve apostles or one of the seventy disciples that propounded the
question is not easy to determine nor is it material to know. Here
Christ gave directions for prayer and a parable about prayer.

He said to them, "Which of you shall have a friend and shall go to
him at midnight and say unto him, 'Friend, lend me three loaves,
for a friend of mine has come to me from a journey, and I have
nothing to set before him.' And from within the house he shall
answer and say, 'Trouble me not, the door is now shut, and my
children are in bed with me. I cannot rise and give to you.' I say
unto you, though he will not rise and give to him because he is his
friend, yet because of his importunity, he will arise and give him as
much as he needs" (Luke 11:5-8). This parable consists of two
parts:

1. A prayer

2. An answer to prayer

In the prayer are four parts:

1. The relation of the person praying to him, namely, his friend. "Which of you shall have a *friend*" (verse 4). Observe that God must be a friend to us before any of our prayers can be accepted.

2. The time of his address is "at midnight" (verse 5), that is, during the time of greatest need and extreme necessity. "With my soul I have desired you in the night" (Isa. 26:9). Observe that the chief time for God's people to be earnest in prayer is a time of trouble.

3. The matter of his request: "Lend me three loaves" (verse 5). Observe that the intent and design of prayer is that we are to order our requests according to our present necessities.

4. The occasion of his request: "A friend has come, and I have nothing" (verse 6).

The answer to this request is double.

1. By way of negation: "Trouble me not" (verse 7). Observe that God's people may have denials to their prayers. The reason for this denial is "the door is now shut, and my children are with me in bed." There are times when God's own people may pray to him, yet he seems to shut his ears to their prayers. God will, as it were, hide from the prayers of his own people. Not only are the doors shut, but his children are in bed with him. The children here are the creatures of God, from which observe: There may be times when God takes away all creature-comforts from his people so that they learn to depend upon Him alone. This is when they are put into the school of importunity.

2. By way of concession: "I say unto you, though he will not rise and give to him because he is his friend, yet because of his importunity, he will arise and give him as much as he needs" (verse 8).

a.) The condition upon which the prayer is answered:

i.) Negatively, he will hear him but not because he is his friend.

ii.) Positively, he will hear him because of his importunity.

Observation 1. A mere state of friendship and reconciliation with God is not always sufficient ground for us to believe that our prayers shall be answered.

Observation 2. At times, there must be a holy importunity, even in God's own friends, to which they expect a gracious return.

b.) Here is the amplification of the concession: There is more given in the concession than was desired in the supplication. He desired but three loaves, and because of his holy importunity, he rose and gave him as much as he needed.

Observe that where there is a holy importunity in our prayers, God does, in his returns to the soul, give more than was desired.

Now, the first part of the text was the relation of the person to whom he made his prayer. The observation is this:

Doctrine 1. Man must be brought into a state of friendship or reconciliation with God before any prayer can be accepted.

I will prove this doctrine by three reasons and then apply it.

1. God accepts not the person for the prayer's sake, but the prayer for the person's sake. We read in Gen. 4:4 that God had respect unto Abel and his offering; first to Abel, then to his sacrifice. God accepted his service because his person was in a state of favor with God. God is first pleased with the person before he can accept the works. This is also laid down in Hebrews. "By faith, Enoch was taken up that he should not see death, for before his being taken up, he had the testimony that he pleased God" (Heb. 11:5). Now,

without faith in Christ to justify your person, you cannot please God. Here lies the great difference between the papists and us. The papists say that works justify the person. We say the person justifies the works. Make the tree good, and the fruit will be good also.

2. Till we are brought into that state of reconciliation, we have no share in the intercession, satisfaction, and righteousness of Jesus Christ, and until we have a share in Him, our prayers cannot be accepted. Jacob could not receive the blessing from his father except in the garments of his elder brother, nor can we receive anything from the hand of God but in the robes of Christ. No prayer can be accepted by God but in and through the intercession of Jesus Christ. If Christ is not an Intercessor in heaven, no prayer will be heard. "There was an angel who came and stood at the altar, having a golden censer, and there was given him incense that he should *offer* it up with the prayers of all saints upon the golden altar which was before the throne" (Rev. 8:3). The word "offer" in the Greek means that he should add it to the prayers of the saints as if the prayers of Christ and a believer were one. God promises, "I will bring my people to my holy mountain and make them joyful in my house of prayer" (Isa. 56:7). In the Hebrew it is, "I will make them joyful in the house of my prayer." Our prayers are as nothing till the intercession of Christ is added to them; without that, they cannot be accepted.

3. Till we are in a state of friendship and reconciliation with God, we do not have the assistance of God's Spirit to help us. If we do not have the assistance of the Spirit, we shall never find acceptance with God. All requests that are not dictated by the Spirit are but the breathings of the flesh which God does not regard. Till we are reconciled to God, we cannot have the Spirit. "Because you are sons, God has sent forth the Spirit of his Son into your hearts, crying, 'Abba Father'" (Gal. 4:6). Till you are sons, you cannot have the Spirit.

And so much for the reasons. I now come to the application.

1. A man must be in a state of friendship before his prayers can be accepted. All that you do before being reconciled to Christ is odious to God, not only your sinful actions, but even your civil, natural, and yes, religious actions. Not that they are so in themselves or in regard of God but in regard of the person who does them. As the psalmist said, "Let his prayer be turned into sin" (Psa. 109:7). Many prayers cannot turn one sin into a grace, but one sin continued in willfully and resolutely can turn all your prayers into sin. "The sacrifice of the wicked is an abomination to the Lord. How much more when he brings it with evil intent" (Prov. 21:27). A diseased body turns that food into corruption while a healthy body turns it into sound nourishment. I have read of a precious stone that had excellent virtue in it but lost all its efficacy if it was put into a dead man's mouth. Prayer is an ordinance of great excellence and efficacy, but if it is in a dead man's mouth, if it comes out of the heart of one that is dead in trespasses and sins, it loses all its virtue. Water that is pure in the fountain is corrupted in the channel.

2. This doctrine overthrows one main pillar of the Roman religion: justification by works. If God accepts the person before he accepts the work, how can any person be justified by works? Unless your person is justified, unless you are reconciled, your works are wicked works. Can wicked works justify? Good works do not make a man good, but a good man makes a work good. Shall a work that a man made good return again and make the man good?

3. Do not look only to the fitness and disposition of your heart in prayer but also to the condition of your soul. It is our duty. It is very good to look to the qualification of the heart in prayer, but the main work is to look after the qualification of the soul and to see whether you are in a state of favor and reconciliation with God. For if your soul is not in favor with God, you may be confident that

11

your petitions will not be heard or accepted. God will look upon your prayers as the corrupt breathings of your sinful heart. You are to examine whether you can go to God in prayer as to a Father. There are many who look after the qualification of their duty in prayer, but few look after the qualification of their person to see whether they are justified or not, whether God is their friend or not. But we should mainly look to this: Let the heart of a man be ever so well composed, yet if your person is not justified, your prayer cannot be accepted. God cares not for the rhetoric of prayers or their eloquence, nor for the arithmetic of prayers (how many they are), nor for the logic of them (how rational and methodical they are), nor for the music of them (what harmony and melody of words you have), but he looks at the holiness of prayer which is from the qualification of a justified person in a sanctified manner. It is good to enquire, "Is my heart right? Is my mind composed? Are my affections raised and kindled in prayer?" But chiefly enquire, "Is my person in a right standing with God through faith in Jesus Christ?"

Let me give a caution: Take heed that you do not mistake this doctrine. Let no man think that because God only accepts the prayers of those who are justified that wicked men are excused from prayer. Though God does not accept every man's prayer, yet every man in the world ought to pray because:

1. They must pray as creatures who stand in need of their Creator. The ravens cry, and God gives them meat.

2. The Lord blames wicked men for not praying to him. "Pour out your wrath upon the nations that do not acknowledge you and upon the families that do not call upon your name" (Jer. 10:25). "There is none that understands, there is none that seeks after God" (Rom 3:11).

3. They are commanded to pray. "Peter said to Simon Magus, 'Repent therefore of this your wickedness, and pray God if perhaps the thoughts of your heart may be forgiven you; for I perceive you are in the gall of bitterness and bonds of iniquity' " (Acts 8:22-23).

Chapter 2

Reasons for Unanswered Prayer

འ

> I say unto you, though he will not rise and give to him because he
> is his friend, yet because of his importunity, he will give him as
> much as he needs.
>
> Luke 11:8

AND so much for first part of the text, namely, the relation between him who prays and the one to whom he prays. I now come to the second part which is the condition upon which the prayer is heard. It is set down in two ways, negatively and positively. The observation is this:

Doctrine 2. A state of friendship or reconciliation with God is not always sufficient to assure a man that God will give returns (or answers) to his prayers. Although a man must be brought into a state of friendship and favor with God before his prayers can be heard, a godly man may make many prayers, yet God may not give an answer to some of his prayers for the following reasons:

1. I shall show the reasons of the doctrine.

2. I shall show in what cases God may refuse to give his own people the things for which they pray.

3. I shall show how we may know when God denies our prayers and whether the denial is in mercy.

The first particular is the reason why God may, and sometimes does, deny to hear the prayers of his friends, and that is this: because God has tied the return of prayer not only to the qualification of the person but also to the qualification of the duty of prayer. The duty must not only be performed by a fit person but also in a right way, in a right manner, to a right end. God does not say, "Let a man pray however he will, I will hear his prayers." That would make him careless and remiss in prayer. Therefore, the Lord expects the qualification of the duty of prayer as well as the qualification of the person. God requires that prayer is done with feeling, fervency, faith, fear, and reverence. It must be done in a right manner.

There is a five-fold qualification that God requires, even of his friends, as a condition to the acceptance of their prayers.

1. *The heart must be prepared.* "Lord, you have heard the desire of the humble, you will prepare their heart, you will cause your ear to hear" (Psa. 10:17). "If you prepare your heart and stretch out your hand towards him; if iniquity is in your hand, put it far away, and let not wickedness dwell in your tabernacle, for then you shall lift up your face without spot; yes, you shall be steadfast and shall not fear" (Job 11:13-15).

2. *Sin must be removed.* So you find in Job 11:13-15, iniquity must be put far away. When God's own people come to worship Him, they must not let any sin lie upon their consciences indulged and unrepented.

3. *The affections must be raised.* When David set himself to prayer he said, "Unto you, O Lord, do I lift up my soul" (Psa. 25:1). You often read in Scripture of lifting up a prayer to God. "It may be the Lord your God will hear the words of Rabshakeh, whom the king of Assyria has sent; therefore, lift up your prayer for the remnant that is left" (Isa. 37:4). "Pray not for this people, neither lift up cry nor prayer for them" (Jer. 11:14). "I will that men pray everywhere, lifting up holy hands, without wrath and doubting" (I Tim. 2:8).

4. *The mind must be composed in prayer* (I Cor. 7:35). We are to attend upon the Lord without distraction. Daniel set his face unto the Lord God to seek Him by prayer and supplications (Dan. 9:3). Likewise, David said, "In the morning, I will direct my prayer unto you" (Psa. 5:3). As an archer who shoots an arrow is careful that his hand does not shake, so the godly man's heart is fixed on God so that he can directly send his prayers to him. Do you think God will hear that prayer which you do not hear yourself? Will God regard that prayer that you do not regard? Will God grant your request when you do not know what you ask because of the distraction that lies upon your spirit? You must take care when you pray that the devil does not distract and disturb you.

5. *The desires must be enlarged after God in prayer.* "Then you shall seek me and find me when you search for me with all your heart" (Jer. 29:13). God bids us to open our mouths wide, and He will fill them (Psa. 18:10). God has not promised to fill the heart unless it is opened.

Now put all these together. Our prayers will not be heard except: 1.) Our hearts are prepared; 2.) Sin is removed; 3.) Our affections are raised; 4.) Our minds are composed; 5.) Our desires for God are enlarged. Judge whether or not this is ground enough for the doctrine that a state of friendship is not sufficient for the acceptance of our prayers.

I come now to the second thing, and that is, a case of conscience: In what cases may God refuse to give his people the things for which they pray? I answer:

1. In case you indulge any sin in the heart. "If I regard iniquity in my heart, the Lord will not hear my prayer" (Psa. 66:18). Sin which is in your heart, by indulgence and approbation, provokes God so that he will not give an answer to your prayers.

2. In case you seek for any mercy from God to be a jewel for your sin and lust. "You ask and receive not because you ask amiss that you may consume it upon your lusts" (Jms. 4:3). So the mother of Zebedee's sons said to Christ, "Grant that these, my two sons, may sit in your kingdom, the one on your right hand and the other on your left" (Matt. 20:21). Now this was an ambitious desire, for she believed Christ would reign upon the earth as an earthly king, and she desired that they might be next to him as he sat upon the throne. Christ said, "You know not what you ask." Christ would not give an answer to her request. He would not gratify her pride and ambition.

3. In case God sees that we are not able to use the mercy well when we have it. If you would ask gifts from God, it may be God sees that enlarged gifts would make you proud, and you would be puffed up and exalt yourself above your brethren. Therefore, God will deny you. We read in Gen. 26:1-2 that when there was a famine in the land, Isaac went to inquire of the Lord whether he should go down to Egypt. God answered, "Do not go down into Egypt." God would not let him go. But in the days of Jacob, there was a famine in the land, and God said to Jacob, "Go down into Egypt." Now what might be the reason that God would have Jacob go down to Egypt and not Isaac? The reason is this: Isaac was a man of weaker graces then Jacob, and God saw that if Isaac had gone down to Egypt for food, he would have fallen into the sins of the land. Now Jacob was a man strong in grace and gifts, for as a prince, he wrestled with God and prevailed, being called Israel. God saw that Jacob would resist their idolatrous ways and not be guilty of their sins. So you may ask mercies of God, but it may be you are not able to manage them well. Therefore, God denies you. But when another asks for the same mercy, God gives it to him because he sees he will use it well and improve it to God's glory. Therefore, reflect upon yourself, and when God denies you a mercy which you

have begged at his hands, say to yourself, "This denial is in mercy, for he did not think me fit for it." If men would take this way to consider God's dealing with them, it would silence all the murmurings and repining of their hearts.

4. If you pray cursorily and carelessly, God may deny you. He who prays coldly, does, as it were, invite God to give him a denial. God promises to be found if we seek him with our whole heart. But if we are careless and regardless, how can we expect that God should regard us?

The third particular is another case of conscience which is this: Seeing that God does not hear the prayers of his people in some cases, how may we know whether the denial of our prayers is in mercy or not? God does not hear the prayers of wicked men. He denies them in wrath. But the prayers of His people are sometimes denied in mercy in the following cases:

1. This is a mercy in case any of his people ask anything that is sinful in itself. God denies his people in mercy that which he gives to others in wrath. God will not always give to his people what they pray for but what is best for them. If God should give his people all they ask, they would be undone. It is a mercy to deny a mad man a sword for he would cut his own throat with it. It is a mercy to deny a child a knife for he would cut his fingers with it. For example, "When Simon Peter saw him, he fell down on his knees, saying, 'Depart from me, for I am a sinful man, O Lord' " (Lk. 5:8). Had Jesus Christ granted Peter his request, he would have been undone forever. Therefore, he would not depart from him. So this denial was in mercy. On the other side, it is a demonstration of God's wrath when God grants mercies to wicked men. So it was with Pharaoh—he desired that God would remove the plagues from him. God granted it, but in wrath, to harden Pharaoh's heart and make him ripe for destruction.

2. God denies us in mercy if what we ask for would be an occasion of sin. Suppose a man begs for wealth, yet God sees that having wealth would make him proud. Now the denial of that is a mercy to him. As in the aforementioned instance, God would not let Isaac go down to Egypt because it would have been an occasion of sin to him. God denies his people in love that which he grants his enemies in anger. God does not grant many in their desires that he may hear them for their good.

3. God denies a prayer in mercy when he gives something better in lieu of it. It was the desire of Moses that he might go into the land of Canaan, but it was better for him to go to the heavenly Canaan; therefore, God translated him there. So the apostles wanted Christ to tell them when he would restore the kingdom to Israel. He would not tell them that, yet he gave them a greater mercy, for he gave them the Holy Spirit. David desired the life of his illegitimate child, but God took it away (which would have been a living monument of David's sin) and gave him Solomon. God will either give us what we ask for (says Bernard) or what he knows to be better for us.

4. God may deny returning this request in mercy to quicken our hearts and affections in prayer and make us more eager in the pursuit after mercy. Many times God denies that mercy which you beg, not as though he would not hear you, but to see how your heart will be drawn out toward him in prayer, to make you more vehement and importunate in your desires. Thus, God was angry with the prayers of his people that they might be more fervent (Psa. 80:4). God does not delay to hear our prayers (says Anselme) because he has no mind to give, but that our desires may be kindled, and so he may take occasion to give more plentifully.

5. God may deny a thing in mercy if you desire it too eagerly and set your heart upon it too affectionately; if you love it too much in the expectation, you will be excessive in the fruition. Rachel wanted

20

children so impetuously that when she had a child, she died in child-bed. God turns requests that are desired too passionately into curses and snares to us, or else He takes them away from us.

Chapter 3

The Necessity of Importunity for Answered Prayer

❧

I say unto you, though he will not rise and give to him because he
is his friend, yet because of his importunity, he will give him as
much as he needs.
Luke 11:8

NOW I come to the positive condition to which answers to prayer
are annexed. Though he will not rise and give to him because he is
his friend, yet because of his importunity, he will rise and give him
as much as he needs. From which part of the text you may observe
this doctrine:

Doctrine 3. The people of God must not content themselves with
being in a state of favor and friendship with God, but they must
also labor after this holy importunity in prayer before they can have
their prayer answered.

In the handling of this doctrine, I shall proceed in this method:

1. I shall answer an objection that stands in the way.

2. I shall show what this importunity is.

    a.) What times God works this in his people

    b.) Wherein lies the difference between a holy importunity and a
natural importunity

c.) What are the reasons why the people of God must have this importunity in prayer

d.) How it comes to pass that so many lack this holy importunity in their prayers

e.) What helps may be used to attain this importunity of spirit

First, I must answer an objection which is this: It may be some will say, "What need is there of importunity in prayer? Has not God decreed what mercy to bestow upon me? If so, then I am sure I shall have those mercies whether I pray or not. On the contrary, if God has not decreed to give me such a mercy, I shall not have it no matter how much I pray for it. For the decree of God is effectual, irresistible, and cannot be altered. All my importunity cannot alter the decree of God."

For an answer to this, I shall propound three things to your consideration:

1. We are not to search into the secret will of God. We are to mind the revealed will of God and not the secret. Our concern should not be to know what God will do but to know what God would have us to do. "The secret things belong to God, but the revealed things to us and to our children" (Deut. 29:29). We know not anything of the decree and counsel of God but only as he is pleased to reveal it.

2. Though God can give a mercy without prayer, yet he has not promised anywhere to give it without prayer. Prayer is the means God has appointed for the obtaining of mercy.

3. The decree of God must not make us remiss in prayer, for God has decreed not only the end but also the means. As God has decreed to give you mercy, so he has also decreed that you should pray for it. Therefore, wherever the decree or purpose of God is

mentioned, it is used as an argument to stir up the people of God to prayer. "For you, O Lord of hosts, God of Israel, have revealed to your servant saying, 'I will build you a house.' Therefore, your servant has found in his heart to pray this prayer unto you. And now, O Lord God, you are God, and your words are true, and you have promised this goodness to your servant. Therefore, let it please you to bless the house of your servant that it may continue forever before you. For you, O Lord God, have spoken it, and with your blessing let the house of your servant be blessed forever" (II Sam. 7:27-29). You see here God had purposed and promised to bless the house of David and to continue it forever. Does this make David remiss in prayer? Does David argue, "What need have I to pray for this mercy, seeing that God is resolved to give it?" No, David takes this hint and uses it to a good purpose in his prayer. Another instance you have in Isaac. God had decreed and promised that the seed of Abraham should be multiplied as the stars of the heaven (Gen. 15:5) and that this promise should be accomplished in Isaac. Did this make Isaac neglect prayer? No, for we read that Isaac entreated the Lord for his wife because she was barren (Gen. 25:21). Though God had promised that in Isaac all the nations of the earth should be blessed, yet Isaac prayed for the accomplishment of that mercy which was decreed and promised.

But you will say, "Suppose God has decreed that he will not give me the mercy for which I pray? What benefit is it for me to pray for it?" I answer:

1. No one knows whether God has decreed that he will deny you the mercy for which you ask.

2. If it is so that God has decreed not to give you the mercy for which you pray, God will give you the return of prayer into your bosom. Though he may not give you the particular thing you desire, he will give something of the same kind.

25

The second particular is: What is this holy importunity? I answer, in general, the word "importunity" in the original signifies impudence or want of shame. It is a metaphor taken from beggars who are impudently importunate and take no denial. If you deny them once, they will ask you again, and again, and never leave till they get what they desire. Importunity is a gathering together of all the affections of the soul, a stirring them all up in prayer, whereby the soul is so earnestly desirous of the good it wants that it will not rest nor leave off the duty until it finds some return or answer to prayer. This is what is meant in Rom. 12:12, "continuing instant in prayer." The original word is very emphatic—it notes not only to persevere but to persevere and continue with utmost strength, to engage all of a man's possibility in the work. It notes urgency and persistence. It is a phrase borrowed from dogs who are on a hunt and will not cease following the game till they catch it. So a godly man will pursue God in prayer and never leave till he finds the mercy he begs from him. Thus Jacob said, "I will not let you go unless you bless me" (Gen. 32:26). So it is said of Elijah that "he prayed earnestly" (Jms. 5:17). In the Greek, it is "in praying, he prayed," to show that a Christian, when he is praying, should yet pray, should pray more earnestly, and should be, as it were, in agony in prayer. It was said of Augustine in his preaching that he never stopped preaching till he found he had done some good upon the hearts of his hearers. So must you pray, and continue praying, and not give up till you find some good done upon your hearts, till you find sin weakened and graces strengthened. This is the holy importunity that is spoken of here.

The third particular is this: When does the Lord work this holy importunity in the hearts of his people? What seasons are the people of God most importunate? I answer:

1. God works this holy importunity in the hearts of his people at their conversion. This is the time when they are most earnest after

God in prayer. Augustine tells us it was so in his time. Converts are most fervent and affectionate toward God in prayer when they are first brought from the state of nature into the state of grace. At the first taste of the excellence of grace, they are much ravished with it because of the newness of the conditions. New things greatly affect men.

2. There is the most holy importunity in a man when he lives under the clearest apprehension and assurance of God's love in Christ. "When I remembered these things, I poured out my soul within me" (Psa. 42:4). When he remembered and considered the marks and tokens of God's grace in him and God's love to him, this made him importunate. A Christian may be compared to a marigold. While the sun shines upon it, it opens itself, but when the sun goes down, it closes itself. When the Sun of God's favor shines upon Christians, their souls are enlarged and their affections are inflamed towards God. But when God hides his face, they are troubled, their hearts are straightened, and they cannot pray as they used to do. It is said of the nightingale that when she thinks anyone is near, she sings more sweetly than when she is alone in the wood. When the soul sees that God is near and full of favor, it sings most sweetly and prays most fervently. But when the love of God is clouded, the soul is left, as it were, alone. The affections flag and grow remiss in prayer.

3. Another time when the people of God are importunate is when the time for the accomplishment of a promise grows near. This we find in Daniel when he understood by the books, according to the word of the Lord through Jeremiah, that he would accomplish seventy years in the desolation of Jerusalem, so he set his face to seek the Lord by prayer and supplication. Daniel prayed at other times, but he was most importunate when the promise was near the accomplishment—then he was most fervent. To the same purpose is Jeremiah, "Then shall you call upon me, and you shall seek for

27

me and find me when you search for me with all your heart" (Jer. 29:13). During the seventy years of exile, the Jews did not express any holy importunity towards God which is the reason for that expression you read in Daniel, "Though all this evil has come upon us, yet we made not our prayer before the Lord our God" (Dan. 9:13). But when the seventy years were drawing near to an end, the Jews prayed more the last year than they did all the seventy years before. Therefore God said, "I know my thoughts that I have towards you, thoughts of peace and not of evil, to give you an expected end. Then shall you call upon me, and shall go and pray unto me, and I will hearken unto you" (Jer. 29:12). Therefore, when you see mercies for a family or a nation lacking, if your heart is indifferent and you do not care whether you pray or not, then you may conclude that mercy will be long before it comes. But if you find that God draws out your heart for mercy; if God stirs up your desires and works this holy importunity in your heart, then it is an argument that mercy is near; for when prayer is in your heart, mercy is at the door.

4. Another time when the people of God are most importunate in prayer is when they are most drawn off from the world and are free from worldly distractions. The same word in the Hebrew signifies both meditation and prayer to show that when the heart has been drawn off from the world by meditation, then it is in a fit posture for prayer.

5. Another time when the people of God are most importunate is when they walk most closely with God. He that lives carelessly will not pray importunately. Therefore Job says, "If iniquity is in your hands, put it away, so you shall lift up your heart" (Job 11:14) to note that iniquity entertained and countenanced in the soul is the great hinderer of prayer and the great cooler of importunity.

6. Another time is in deep and bitter afflictions. This is when the people of God are most importunate in their prayers. "Out of the deeps have I cried unto you; Lord, hear the voice of my supplication" (Psa. 130:1-2). "I cried unto the Lord with my voice. I poured out my complaint before him; I showed him my trouble" (Psa. 142:1-2). "They cried unto the Lord in their trouble" (Psa. 107:6). When trouble and great distress were upon the Jews by Sennacherib, it was said, "For this cause Hezekiah the king, and the prophet Isaiah, the son of Amos, prayed and cried to heaven" (II Chr. 32:20). So it was said of Manasseh, "When he was in affliction, he sought the Lord his God and humbled himself greatly and prayed" (II Chr. 33:12). So it was said by Hannah, "I am a woman of a sorrowful spirit and have poured out my soul before the Lord" (I Sam. 1:15). Thus it was with the whole Church. "With my soul I have desired you in the night; yes, with my spirit within me I will seek you early; for when your judgments are abroad, the inhabitants of the world will learn righteousness" (Isa. 26:9). That is the last season wherein the people of God are importunate with God in prayer.

Chapter 4

Characteristics of Importunity

ॐ

I say unto you, though he will not rise and give to him because he
is his friend, yet because of his importunity, he will give him as
much as he needs.
Luke 11:8

THE fourth particular is this: What is the difference between the
holy importunity in God's people and the seeming importunity
which flows from the gifts of nature?

Answer: It lies in these seven things.

1. A holy importunity makes a man restless till his prayers are heard.
"I stretch forth mine hands unto you. My soul thirsts after you as a
thirsty land; hear me speedily, my spirit fails; hide not your face
from me, lest I am like them that go down into the pit" (Psa. 143:6-
7). As a thirsty land is never satisfied till it gets rain, so "my soul is
crushed with longing after your law" (Psa. 119:20), and "as the deer
pants after the water brooks, so pants my soul after you, O God"
(Psa. 42:1). The deer never rests, it never gives over running till it
comes to the water. Such is the importunity of a godly man—he is
never quiet, never satisfied, till his prayers are returned into his
bosom. But it is otherwise with a hypocrite. He prays for mercy and
pardon of sin, but he can rest contented when God does not hear
him. He can beg for grace, but he can be very well satisfied without
grace. "The soul of the sluggard desires and has nothing, but the
soul of the diligent is fat" (Prov. 13:4).

2. A holy importunity is known by this: It makes a man more earnest for spiritual mercies than temporal mercies. This has been the temper of God's people. "There be many that say, 'Who will show us any good?' But Lord, lift up the light of your countenance upon us" (Psa. 4:6). Observe the difference between David's temper and that of the wicked: Their great question and desire was who would show them any good, who would give them the increase of corn and wine. But David's heart breathed after other things, after God's favor and the light of his countenance. So "I stretch forth mine hands unto you, my soul thirsts after you" (Psa. 143:6-8). "O God, you are my God, early will I seek you; my soul thirsts for you, my flesh longs for you in a dry and thirsty land where there is no water" (Psa. 63:1). David was in a wilderness. He wanted water. One would have thought that he should have sought God for water. But you see, David's desires ran in another channel. He thirsted more for God than for water. He desired spiritual advantages more than temporal enjoyments. This importunity makes a man endeavor more against sin than affliction. It makes him desire God's grace more than common mercies. But now the heart of a hypocrite is more desirous of temporal mercies than spiritual mercies. You read in Hosea, "They have not cried unto me with their heart when they howled upon their beds. They assemble themselves for corn and wine, and they rebel against me" (Hos. 7:14). They howled for what? Was it for grace and spiritual blessings? No, it was for corn and wine, not for grace, not for acquaintance with God. Another instance you have in Acts with Simon Magus who offered money to purchase the Holy Spirit. What was his end in desiring the Holy Spirit? Was it to obtain a spiritual mercy? No, it was that he might work miracles. When Peter told him to beg for spiritual mercy, Simon Magus did not follow Peter's instruction. He had no great desire for pardon of sin or any spiritual mercy, but he prayed that none of those things which Peter had spoken might come upon him. That is, that his money might

not perish, nor he perish with it—that his gifts might not perish. This was his great request and desire.

3. A holy importunity of God's people consists more of inward affections rather than just outward expressions. "All my desire is before you, and my groanings are not hid from you" (Psa. 38:9). David's heart panted and failed him (ver. 10), but he did not have a word of expression, though his expressions were very good. "The Spirit helps our infirmities with sighs and groans that cannot be uttered" (Rom. 8:26). It is said, "The four and twenty elders had golden vials full of odors which are the prayers of the saints" (Rev. 5:8). They are called odors for their sweetness, golden for their excellence, and vials, which are vessels of large extent in the belly but narrow-mouthed. The hearts of God's people are like vials many times enlarged when they are straightened in their words and expressions. Dilated desires exist in the hearts of the saints, yet the saints are so narrow-mouthed that they are not able to utter them. It is otherwise with hypocrites. They have more in the expression than in the heart. It was God's complaint against the Jews of old, "They draw near to God with their lips when their hearts are far from him" (Isa. 29:13). A hypocrite performs duties, but his duties never reach his heart. They are like a pot that is hot at the top but cold at the bottom.

4. A holy importunity makes a man more enlarged before God in secret than before men in public. "O my dove who is in the clefts of the rock, in the secret places of the mountainside, let me see your countenance, let me hear your voice, for sweet is your voice and your countenance is comely" (Cant. 2:14). The voice of Christ's church is sweet even when she is in secret, when none but God beholds her. "You that dwell in the gardens, the companions hearken to your voice; cause me to hear it" (Cant. 8:13). But a hypocrite does not care to have any secret communion with God. He does not care to pray alone. And if he is brought to that, he

takes no care for his heart. He does not curb his thoughts. All his care is in company, popular applause, and vain-glory, which like wind to the sails of a ship make his affections move faster. A hypocrite, in this regard, may resemble a nightingale which sings sweetest when any man stands near. So carnal men, when others are witnesses of their actions, put forth the utmost of their ability. They are of John's temper—he was zealous only upon the condition that others would see it.

5. This holy importunity makes a godly man more humble. The reason is because he looks upon his enlargements in prayer, not as coming from the strength of his natural parts or abilities, but as the free gift and gracious dispensation of God's Spirit. He sees that he has nothing to boast of and so it makes himself low in his own eyes. You know that a violet is one of the sweetest flowers, and it grows lowest in the earth. The fullest ears of corn do hang down the most. The fullest barrels make the least noise. So the gracious heart is most low and vile in its own apprehensions, being nearest the earth like dust and ashes. The fuller he is of divine discoveries or enlargements, the less boasting he makes in the world. A ship, the heavier it is laden, the less it is tossed with winds and waves. The more empty it is, the more it is lifted up above the water. So it is with man—the more empty he is of divine discoveries, the more he is tossed to and fro with every wind of applause. Grace is, as it were, the ballast of the soul to keep down a man's spirits and make him humble in the midst of wit and parts. "Be therefore sober and watchful in prayer" (I Peter 4:7). Be sober and not puffed up. Do not boast of your enlargements. Though it is true that it refers to another thing, yet the principle refers to prayer. The man that prays with most enlargedness of affections towards God must watch over his spirit and be sober. Sobriety is opposed to pride, for a man ought to have humility concerning his own gifts and graces. Watchfulness is opposed to remissness, deadness, and carelessness

of spirit in the performance of duties. Thus it is with a sincere man who has this true importunity in him. But now wicked men, if ever they have enlargements in duty, they are puffed up. It is with them as it was with Uzziah. "God had helped him marvelously till he was strong. But when he was strong, his heart was lifted up to his destruction" (II Chr. 26:16). When God helps the soul of such a man in duty, he is tempted to lift himself up against God and be puffed up above his brethren.

6. He whose desires are quickened rather than abated by denials has this holy importunity in him. You find this in the woman of Canaan. "She cried unto Christ saying, 'Have mercy on me, O Lord, Son of David. My daughter is grievously vexed with a devil' " (Matt. 15:22). Jesus took no notice of her. He answered her not a word (ver. 23). There is one discouragement. It seems that she would have ceased asking at this point, but she prayed again, and the disciples begged him to send her away (ver. 23). That was another discouragement which would have knocked off the desires of many, but she continued her request still. Then Jesus answered her, "I am not sent but to the lost sheep of the house of Israel" (ver. 24). This is a third discouragement, and yet this did not cool her affections but stirred her to come afresh to Christ once again. She came and worshipped, saying, "Lord, help me" (ver. 25). Yet she found another rebuff and that worse than any of the former. Jesus said, "It is not good to take the children's bread and give it to dogs" (ver. 26). Christ, you see, called her a dog, and yet all this did not cast her off, but she took encouragement even from this discouraging answer. And she said, "True, Lord, yet even the dogs eat of the crumbs which fall from their master's table" (ver. 27). She was resolved that she would not give over till she got what she came for, till Christ had said, "O woman, great is your faith. Be it unto you even as you will" (ver. 28). Denials are to the saints as water to the smiths-forge when it is sprinkled upon it. It is so far

from cooling or quenching that it makes it burn with greater heat. So the denials and discouragements that God's people meet with serve as bellows to blow up the sparks within to a flame, to make their desires stronger and their affections burn the hotter. But to a hypocrite, denials and discouragements take off the wheels of his affections. "What is the Almighty that we should serve him, and what profit should we have if we pray unto him?" (Job 21:15). We get no good by it. The mercies we ask are not yet in our hands. Now this argues a sinful impatience and lack of holy importunity.

7. Holy importunity is kindled in the heart by the motions and operations of God's blessed Spirit. "Because you are sons, God has sent forth the Spirit of his Son into your hearts, crying, 'Abba, Father' " (Gal. 4:6). In the time of the law, the sacrifices accepted by God were burnt with fire from heaven. "There came fire out from before the Lord, and it consumed the burnt-offering upon the altar" (Lev. 9:24). "When Elijah had laid his sacrifice upon the altar of the Lord, then the fire of the Lord fell and consumed the burnt sacrifice and the wood" (I Kgs. 18:38). So the heathen's vestal-flames were kindled with sunbeams. The true importunity that is from above is a fire kindled by God himself in the hearts of his people. But there is another importunity that comes from natural principles, natural abilities, a strong memory, a profound judgment, a ready wit, and a fluent tongue. While these are very advantageous to the duty, they are not an indicator of holy importunity. There is the gift of prayer as well as the grace of prayer. Some are importunate in prayer out of fleshly respects. Now this is but a counterfeit importunity.

Chapter 5

Why Believers Must Labor for Importunity in Prayer

❧

I say unto you, though he will not rise and give to him because he
is his friend, yet because of his importunity, he will give him as
much as he needs.

Luke 11:8

THE fifth particular is this: What are the reasons why God's people
must labor for this holy importunity in their prayers?

First, I answer, because God has promised returns or answers, not
to the persons praying, but to the qualifications of their prayers.
And when the Scripture makes mention of this duty of prayer, it
also makes mention of several concomitants that must go along
with it to make it acceptable. For instance, there are diverse
concomitants which the Scripture holds forth to be necessary for
the acceptance of our prayers.

1. You must pray believingly. "He that comes to God must believe"
(Heb. 11:4). Jesus says, "Therefore I say unto you, whatever things
you desire when you pray, believe that you receive them and you
shall have them" (Mark 11:24). He does not say pray how you will
and you shall have it, but *pray believingly*, and you shall receive. James
said, "If any man lacks wisdom, let him ask it of God. But let him
ask in faith, not wavering, for he that wavers is like a wave of the
sea driven with the wind and tossed" (Jms. 1:5-6). So you see, God
looks to the manner as well as to the matter of prayer.

37

2. You must pray regularly, according to the will of God.

3. You must pray dependently, resting upon Christ's intercession.

4. You must pray patiently, waiting on the Lord for an answer.

5. You must pray preparedly.

6. You must pray earnestly, fervently, and importunately as David. "I will pray and cry aloud, and he shall hear my voice" (Psa. 55:17). A full place to this purpose is Rom. 15:30, "Now I beseech you, brethren, for the Lord Jesus Christ's sake and for the love of the Spirit, that you strive together with me in your prayers to God for me." The word in the Greek is very emphatic—it is the same word that is applied to Christ when he was in an agony and sweat great drops of blood. He beseeches them to contend and strive in their prayers. We are to be, as it were, in agony when we are in prayer. Prayer is not a little book labor; it is not a lip-labor only, but it is a raising up and putting forth the heart and affections in the work. So Rom. 12:12, "continuing instant in prayer," is a metaphor taken from dogs. A dog of all creatures is best able to endure hunger. He will run from place to place and never leave till he catches his prey. So you are to hunger after God, and after mercy, and not rest till God grants you the mercy you stand in need of. Pray and pray and pray again, and fight till you overcome. Pray till you get an answer. Another example can be found in James. "The effectual *fervent* prayer of a righteous man avails much" (Jms. 5:16). The word in the original is significant. Some expound it a "working prayer." It may be interpreted as a prayer well-wrought in the heart, and so, a prayer that comes from the heart. It is prayer wrought in us by the Spirit and carried on by faith. Another place to the same purpose is Acts 26:7, "Unto which promise our twelve tribes hope to attain as they *earnestly* serve God day and night." The word is rendered by some "continually, daily, constantly," but it signifies most properly a serving of God with the utmost of one's strength, to be as a man

upon a rack and to use all of his power. Or it may be borrowed from one that runs a race wherein a man stretches out his limbs to the utmost. The same word is used in Acts 12:5, "prayer was made *without ceasing*," or as it is in the margin of your book, and more agreeable to the original, "instant and earnest prayer" was made for Peter. The prayers of God's people were so earnest that they opened the prison doors for him. So Col. 4:12, "Epaphras, who is one of you, a servant of Christ, salutes you, always *laboring* fervently for you in prayers." In the Greek, this word literally means, "to agonize" in prayer. So you see, it is not every prayer that God is satisfied with, but it is the fervent prayer that shall prevail with God.

Second, we must have this holy importunity in prayer because there is much strength against you when you go upon your knees. There is strength against you from without and from within.

1. There is strength against us from without. There are the powers of darkness that stand against you and resist you, as it was with Abraham. "When Abraham was sacrificing, birds came down upon the sacrifice, but Abraham drove them away" (Gen. 15:11). Deodate says this is a sign that the devils labor to disturb us in holy duties. As the good angels behold us in our assemblies and rejoice to see our order, so the wicked angels labor to disturb us and molest us.

2. There is strength against us from within. There is in your heart that which will carry you more violently from God than good motions can bring you to God. There is a forcible withdrawing of the heart from God. "Every man is tempted when he is drawn away of his own lust and enticed" (Jms. 1:14). When you have no will to do good, then you have the will to do evil; nay, there are wills of the flesh and lusts of the flesh. Shall we not have half a will for God when we have so many wills for sin? You see, therefore, it is not without good reason that we should be importunate in prayer.

39

The sixth particular is this: What are the reasons why so many people lack this holy importunity? Why do so many pray and so few pray with that earnestness and eagerness of heart that is required? I answer that it comes to pass for many reasons.

1. This comes to pass from the injections and instigations of Satan. The devil not only acts powerfully but subtly and craftily. He will endeavor to divert you from the performance of duty. He will persuade you to neglect it if he can. It may be that you will say that you direct your prayers to God and have your eyes fixed upon him. Why, now, Satan will fall in with you, he will jog your arm, he will take your eye off the mark that you shall not be able to hit it. Thus, he dealt with Abraham as you heard before. Thus, he dealt with Job. "Now there was a day when the sons of God came to present themselves before the Lord, and Satan came also among them" (Job 1:6). I am not ignorant that many interpreters understand the phrase "sons of God" to refer to angels because the angels are called the sons of God in Job 38:7. But it cannot be so taken here. I will give but one reason to prove it—because the place where the angels are is in heaven, and if so, then the devil must be in heaven, which is denied by all. He never was in heaven since he was cast out of it. Bolducius said that this day was the Lord's Day, and the phrase "sons of God" means the godly men that lived in the time and place where Job lived, namely, the posterity of Seth. You shall find in Scripture this very appellation given to them in Gen. 6:2, "The sons of God saw the daughters of men." These sons of God must be men and not angels, and so they are to be understood in this place in Job. The people of God met together and came before the Lord, and Satan also came among them to hinder them and disturb them. So it was in Zech. 3:1-2, "And he showed me Joshua the High Priest standing before the Angel of the Lord and Satan standing at his right hand to resist him. And the Lord said unto Satan, 'The Lord rebuke you, O Satan, even the Lord that has

chosen Jerusalem rebuke you. Is not this a firebrand plucked out of the fire?'" You see how Satan labored to divert the thoughts and distract the heart of the High Priest in the performance of religious duties.

2. This importunity is wanting in our prayers when we know and allow ourselves in any one sin and let it lie upon our hearts without repenting. Hildersham gathers from the 51st psalm that the entire time David was in the sin of adultery, his heart was shut up so that he could not pray as he did before nor pray as he did after he had repented of that sin. You need to look to your hearts to see that there is no sin there of which you have not repented. For be sure of this, if your prayer does not make you stop sinning, your sin will make you stop praying.

3. Another reason that importunity is lacking in our prayers is because many do not pray at the right time. It is the judgment of that learned and reverend man of God, Mr. Bolton, that the taking of unfit time for prayer does more to obstruct and hinder this holy importunity in prayer than all the suggestions and instigations of Satan.

Now, there are three unfit seasons for prayer:

1. When the body is sleepy and fit for nothing but to take its rest. A sleepy and sluggish temper is a canker to eat out many sweet affections for God. "By night upon my bed I sought him, but I found him not" (Cant. 3:1). Some interpreters take occasion here to speak against late prayers.

2. Another unfit season is when the heart is filled with worldly care, distractions, and the encumbrances of this present life. Many men are guilty of this. They so clog themselves with the cares of this life that they cannot pray without distraction. Some men will be down upon their knees before the things of this world are out of their

41

minds, and so they have no time to consider, meditate, or put the heart into a fit frame for that work of prayer. You know we are to attend upon the Lord without distraction (I Cor. 7:35). It was the fault of those Jews that when they came to hear the word of the Lord their hearts went out after covetousness (Ezek. 33:31).

3. Another unfit season for prayer is when we are under passionate distempers. When tumultuous passions are up, holy affections are down. "I will that men pray everywhere, lifting up holy hands without wrath and doubting" (I Tim. 2:8). This is to show that where there is wrath, the duty of prayer cannot be performed in an acceptable manner. Of the same mind was the apostle Peter who therefore gave this counsel: "Likewise, husbands, dwell with your wives according to knowledge, giving honor as unto the weaker vessel and as being heirs together of the grace of life that your prayers be not hindered" (I Pet. 3:7). The apostle wisely foresaw that if a man and his wife lived in discontent and trouble, their prayers would be hindered. Therefore, he advises them to prevent the hindrance of their prayers by avoiding occasions of discontent.

That is the third season wherein people are unfit for prayer, diverting them from that fervency and importunity they should have in their prayers. Therefore, we should choose the fittest seasons for prayer. It is said by Vitus Theodorus, who overheard Luther's private prayers many times, "There was not a day that passed over his head wherein Luther did not spend three hours, at the least, in prayer, and those were not hours that he could best spare. They were unseasonable hours but such hours as were the fittest for his study. . . . With how much reverence did I hear him pray! With how much boldness and confidence!" On the contrary, one reason why men have so little of this holy importunity is lack of making time for the work of prayer.

4. Another reason for the lack of holy importunity is the irregularity and neglect of prayer in your Christian course. Many there are who pray sometimes and then leave off praying again. Now this significantly dulls men's affections in prayer. There is a proverb, "use makes perfection." I am sure it is so in the duty of prayer. Let a Christian pray often, and he will come to pray well and to pray with much enlargedness of heart. But let him leave off prayer, and he will find his heart exceedingly straightened. Take a key—if you use it frequently, it will be bright, but if you lay it aside, it will soon grow rusty. Thus, it will be with a man's heart. Be frequent in prayer, and your heart will be bright. Let the key of prayer that opens heaven be used, and your prayer will enter into heaven. But let this key of prayer be laid aside, and it will quickly grow rusty. Your prayers and performances will not be able to enter heaven, and you will not be able to pray in the manner God expects. If you do not watch and pray, you will lose your holy desires after God. As it is with a water pump, if you use it every day, water will come. But if you forbear the use of it two or three days, water will neither come so easily nor so plentifully. If you do not pump out your holy desires every day, they will quickly flag and grow remiss. Physicians observe concerning the teeth that the side of the tooth that is not used is most subject to rheumes and distillations. The heart that is not devoted to prayer is most subject to Satan's temptations and suggestions.

5. The fifth reason why this importunity is lacking is because men tie themselves to prescript forms of prayer. I do not say that it is unlawful to use set forms of prayer. We find that Jesus Christ himself used a form. He said, "Father, if it is possible, let this cup pass from me" (Matt. 26:39). He went again the second time and prayed saying, "O my Father, if this cup may not pass from me, thy will be done." He went away and prayed again, saying the same

words. This is to show that it is lawful to use forms of prayer, but not always.

You are to strive for the spirit of prayer. A man that will constantly use his crutches shall go lame all the days of his life. We live in an age wherein religion is professed and the gospel is fully known. Do not content yourselves with forms. Labor for the spirit of prayer. You may go to God and spread before him your wants and necessities, and you may ask for those mercies that are most suitable to your wants and exigencies. Forms indeed will teach you to beg pardon for sin, in general, but you must beg pardon for sins in particular. You must not only beg mercy in general, but you must beg particular mercies that are most pertinent to you. He that ties himself to another man's form of prayer will not be able to pray alone, and when he does, it will be weak, cold, and formal.

6. This sixth reason why importunity is lacking is that many give way to carelessness in prayer. This incapacitates the affections and emasculates the spirits. What men are accustomed to doing, they get a habit of doing so that they cannot do the contrary. For example, a carrier's horse that is used to a dull and slow pace cannot get out of it. The lessening of acts makes habits more remiss.

Chapter 6

How to Attain Importunity

෨

I say unto you, though he will not rise and give to him because he is his friend, yet because of his importunity, he will give him as much as he needs.
Luke 11:8

THE sixth particular is this: By what helps may a man attain this holy importunity in prayer? For an answer, I shall lay down six or seven theological helps by which a man may come to attain this holy importunity.

1. Possess your heart with a lawful fear of the Almighty God. This was the ground of David's importunity. "My voice you shall hear in the morning. . . . But as for me, I will come into your house, in the multitude of your mercy; and in your fear, I will worship toward your holy temple" (Psa. 5:3, 7). David came to duty with a strong sense of God's greatness and dreadfulness. So it is the advice of the apostle that if we would serve God acceptably, we must do it "with reverence and godly fear" (Heb. 12:28). That forecited author, Vitus Theodorus, wrote concerning Luther, "He prayed with so much confidence as if he had been speaking with his friend and familiar, and yet with so much reverence as one that considered the great distance between God and himself." I may allude to that place in Isaiah, though the words are spoken to another purpose, "Your heart shall fear and be enlarged" (Isa. 60:5). A holy fear breeds holy care. If a man comes to the point of not fearing God, he will quickly be careless in prayer. "Yes, you cast off fear and restrain prayer before God" (Job 15:4). A man that casts off the fear of God soon

ceases to pray to God. He that fears God most will certainly pray to God best. That is the first help.

2. Another help or means to get this holy importunity is this: Recollect your thoughts by holy meditation before you come to this weighty duty of prayer. Upon this ground, we find meditation and prayer to be put together. "Give ear to my words, O Lord, and consider my meditation; give ear unto my prayer, O my God and my King, for unto you will I pray" (Psa. 5:1-2). David's prayer, you see, is ushered in with meditation. The same word in the Hebrew signifies both to meditate and to pray. You find this concerning Isaac (Gen. 24:26). Isaac went out into the fields to meditate, or as some translate it, "to pray." It is likely he did both—first he meditated, then he prayed. Be much employed in the work of meditation if you would have your hearts much enlarged in prayer. Meditate upon whose presence you are entering and what a glorious God he is. Meditate in whose name you are coming and by whom you must have access to the throne of grace. Meditate upon what chief mercies you want and what grace you would have strengthened, what lusts you would have quelled, what doubts you would have satisfied, what sins you would have pardoned, in a word, what blessings you would have God bestow upon you. The meditation of these things will give a man more capacity and fire to his affections in prayer.

3. If you would get this holy importunity, you must withdraw your thoughts from worldly cares and distractions. The apostle Paul exhorts the believers in Corinth to free themselves from the cares of the world, and he gives this as a reason: that they may attend upon the Lord without distraction. The cares of the world will eat out the good that is in the heart of man, robbing him of that freedom and enlargement that he otherwise might have in prayer. Anselm, as he was walking in the fields, saw a shepherd's boy tie a stone to a bird's leg. As the bird sought to fly up, the stone started

46

to pull him down again. The spiritual interpretation we may make is this: When the soul would mount aloft in prayer and grow fervent, the cares of the world pluck it down and cool it. Therefore, you must labor to free yourselves from these encumbrances. You must do as Abraham did when he went to sacrifice—he left his servants and cattle at the bottom of the hill. So when you go to offer God the sacrifices of prayer, you must get above the impediments and distractions of this present life.

4. Another way to get this holy importunity is to watch the heart in prayer. "Continue in prayer, and watch in the same with thanksgiving" (Col. 4:2). There is a watching to prayer and a watching in prayer. A watching to prayer is when a man watches his heart and sees that he does not omit the duty of prayer. A watching in prayer, of which I am now speaking, is guarding the heart while praying.

Now there are four enemies that a man must watch against in prayer.

a.) Watch against drowsiness of body. This is a great impediment of prayer, and we have great need to watch against it.

b.) Watch against a deadness and dullness of spirit, against a flat and low temper that is a great hindrance of importunity.

c.) Watch against satanical suggestions. Satan is always ready to assault you. He watches to disturb and assault you in your prayers. You must watch to counter-work him.

d.) You must watch from secular distractions. All these adversaries you must watch against, and that is the way to get this holy importunity into your hearts.

5. If you would get this holy importunity, you must labor to stir up your affections when you come to pray. This you find was the

practice of holy David. "Bless the Lord, O my soul, and all that is within me, bless his holy name" (Psa. 103:1). See how this good man musters together all the faculties of his soul, how he calls up all his strength, all that he can do to set forth the name of God? So Peter exhorts believers to gird up the loins of their minds (I Pet. 1:13). A Christian going towards heaven is compared to a man that is going on a journey. Now a man that is going on a journey girds up his clothes about his loins that nothing may hinder him in his journey. The Apostle alludes to this when he bids them to gird up their loins. So you have in Luke 17:8, "Gird up yourself, and serve me." It is an expression of a master to his servant. God is our master, and we are his servants. We are to do his work while we are in the world. To that end, let us gird up our loins and gather our affections together that we may be more fit and more vigorous in the work. A distinct and ungirded mind is not fit for prayer. In ancient times, at the first assembly and church meetings, the deacons cried, "Let us pray! Let us attend!" There are many who pray but do not attend to prayer. Many pray as if they prayed not; if therefore we would pray, we must attend to it—we must stir up all that is within us to call upon the name of the Lord.

6. If you would get this holy importunity, then you must store your hearts with fullness of matter when you go to prayer. It is emptiness of spirit that causes deadness of heart.

7. If you would get this holy importunity, bemoan the deadness and dullness of your heart. This was the course that David took. "My desires, O Lord, are before you, and my groaning is not hidden from you" (Psa. 38:9). So it was the practice of the church. "O Lord, why have you made us err from your ways and hardened our hearts from your fear?" (Isa. 63:17). So it was with Ephraim. "I have heard Ephraim bemoaning himself. You have chastised me, and I was chastised as a bullock unaccustomed to the yoke. Surely after that I was turned, I repented, and after that I was instructed, I smote upon

my thigh. I was ashamed, yes, even confounded, because I did bear the reproach of my youth" (Jer. 31:18-19). God loves to hear his people mourning over and bewailing their wants and weaknesses. That is one necessary requisite in an acceptable prayer. Bewail your dullness. Consider that prayer without this holy importunity is like a messenger without legs or an arrow without feathers or an advocate without a tongue. Jerome complained of his distractions and dullness in prayer, chiding himself saying, "Do you think that Jonah prayed liked this when he was in the whale's belly, or Daniel when he was among the lions, or the thief when he was upon the cross?" If you would get this importunity, bemoan your lack of importunity, and so much shall suffice for the helps or means to get importunity. Now that I have dispatched all those particulars propounded in the beginning, I come to the application of the point. I shall apply it by way of caution to prevent several mistakes about this holy importunity. There are two sorts of mistakes. There are some who think they have this importunity when they do not have it, and there are others who think they do not have it when indeed they do. Both of these mistakes I must labor to rectify.

First, there are some who think they have this importunity when they do not have it. Every man by nature is proud of his own parts and abilities, and he is apt to think that he has more grace than he has. Here are four mistakes, or if you will, four grounds of this great mistake. Many believe they have this importunity when indeed they do not have it. They think they have it because:

1. They are fluent in their expressions in prayer.

2. They have some stirring of affections in prayer.

3. God gives them the mercy for which they ask.

4. They pray by heart and not by book.

Now all of these are false grounds. Therefore, I shall endeavor to disprove them in order. The *first* ground of this deceit is this: There are some who believe they have this importunity because they have a multitude of words and a variety of expressions in prayer. Now this is no just ground for a man to conclude that he has this holy importunity in four cases:

1. In the case when expressions come from natural gifts and abilities and not from saving grace, it is a sign that you do not have this holy importunity. A man may have a strong memory, volubility of tongue, and good natural abilities, and yet all of this falls far short of this gracious importunity.

2. In the case when you are full in expression but empty in affection, it is a sign that you do not have this holy importunity. There are many men whose words out-slip their hearts, and their expressions exceed their affections. "For as much as this people draw near to me with their mouths, and with their lips do honor me, yet they have removed their hearts far from me" (Isa. 29:13). Some men are like boiling water when it boils out of the top of the pot, but there is nothing at the bottom. All their prayers are at the top, in their mouth, and not in their hearts and affections. Their affections do not carry equipage with their words.

3. In the case when your importunate expressions are used more in the presence of others than in secret, it is a sign that you do not have this holy importunity. Instead, you have the desire for popular applause. It is not so with the people of God. Christ speaks to his people, "You that dwell in the gardens, the companions hearken to your voice, cause me to hear it" (Cant. 8:13) to show that they should not only pray and be importunate when they are in company, but when no eye sees them, when no ear hears them, when none is present but God alone. God expects that we should pray in secret as well as in company.

4. In the case when your fluency of expressions makes you conceited of yourself and your gifts, causing you to slight the gifts of other men—this is an argument that you do not have this holy importunity, for a holy importunity makes a man humble and low in his own eyes. When a man comes to despise other men and exalt himself above his brethren, this is a token that your importunity does not come not from a right principle.

The second false ground upon which men believe they have this importunity is because they find in themselves some stirring of their affections in prayer. But this is no just ground for that opinion in these cases:

1. In the case when your affections are more stirred up for the removal of affliction rather than the corruption within you, it is a sign that you do not have this holy importunity. It was so with the mariners in Jonah. They cried mightily unto God, but for what? It was not that they might be delivered from their sins and corruptions but that God would bring them safely out of that tempest wherein they were afflicted.

2. In the case when your affections are kindled by a false principle such as popular applause or vain glory, and not by the Spirit of God, it is a sign that you do not have this holy importunity.

3. In the case when your affections are more drawn out after pardoning mercy than subduing grace, it is a sign that you do not have this holy importunity. A man whose conscience is awakened may be so far roused with the fear of hell that he may be very earnest to have sin pardoned out of a mere principle of self-love.

4. In the case when these stirrings are fading, it is a sign that you do not have this holy importunity. There are many who have a flushing in their affections but have no continuing affections in their hearts. They are like a man in a fever—when the distemper is on him, he

51

may be far stronger than he is in his ordinary course. Now this is not the natural strength of the man but only the violence of his distemper and the decay of his nature. Just so, the violence that some men have does not argue a strength of grace but a decrease of grace.

A third ground upon which many mistake that they have this holy importunity is this: because God gives them the mercy they ask. They think God would not give them what they ask if he did not hear and accept their prayers. But neither is this a good ground and for these reasons:

1. God may give you mercy not as a return of prayer but as a fruit of his general providence whereby he takes care of all his creatures. God gives meat even to ravens that cry unto him. The Lord gives to everything their meat in due season. God hears the cries of the lowest of all his creatures in the time of need.

2. God may hear you and grant your request in wrath and not in mercy. So it was with the Israelites. They were weary of that government that God had set over them, and they were very importunate to have a king. Nothing would satisfy them but a king. They refused to hear the voice of Samuel and said, "No, but we will have a king." Well, God heard their request and gave them a king. Might they have concluded that their prayers were accepted because God gave them what they desired? No. God said, "I gave you a king in my anger" (Hos. 13:11). Likewise, the Israelites were very desirous of meat, and God heard them. "So they did eat and were filled, for he gave them their own desire" (Psa. 78:29-31). They were not estranged from their lust, but while the meat was in their mouths, the wrath of God came upon them and slew the fattest of them and smote down the chosen men of Israel. So God's granting a man what he asks is not necessarily a reason to conclude that God accepts his prayers.

3. If God has heard you, it may be it is in temporal favors but not spiritual mercies. God gives you a temporal mercy, but he denies you spiritual mercies. It may be you have begged riches, and God has granted you this request to make you rich in the world. It may be you have desired honor, and you are raised to places of honor. But remember, you are to beg for Christ, to beg grace, to beg for His glory. If God does not give you these, you shall never see the face of God. Consider what good will riches and honors do you then? They will but make you fat for the day of slaughter and make you a sweet morsel for worms and devils. Now consider what benefit it is to have riches, pleasures, and worldly enjoyments when they prove a snare to you. So it is no just ground for a man to conclude that he has prayed aright because God has answered him.

The fourth ground of man's presumption of the acceptableness of his prayers is this: he prays by heart and not by book; he does not use set forms but prays extempore. But this also is a false ground as appears by these considerations:

1. It is possible for a man to pray without book yet without heart, too. He may pray by the strength of natural parts, as I told you before.

2. A man may pray without form and yet make a formal prayer. A formal prayer is not the use of a form of words, for that Jesus Christ did. He prayed three times saying the same words. A man may possibly use a form of words and yet not be formal. On the other hand, a man may be formal and not use a form of words. That is, he may pray and yet not have his heart and affections wrought upon in that prayer.

3. Prayer is not a work of the memory, invention, or expression but a work of the heart. Prayer does not consist in a variety of phrases or a change of the method and expression used in prayer but a work on the affections. God does not account that to be a prayer that

does not come from the heart and is not accompanied with the heart. Therefore, you find this expression concerning the saints' prayers. Hannah poured out her soul before the Lord (I Sam. 1:15). The psalmist is said to have poured out his heart (Psa. 142:2). The Israelites are said to have poured out their hearts like water before the Lord (Lam. 2:19). So trusting in one's form or lack of form in prayer proves to be a false bottom.

Chapter 7

Comfort for the Discouraged

ॐ

I say unto you, though he will not rise and give to him because he
is his friend, yet because of his importunity, he will give him as
much as he needs.
Luke 11:8

SECOND, there are many who have this holy importunity but do
not think that they have it. They say, "Others pray better than I,"
and "Others pray with more enlargedness of heart than I." Now
this reasoning is not good.

1. It may be those whom you think pray better than you are of
longer standing and larger experience in the ways of God than you.
God does not expect any more from a man but according to that
measure of grace he gives the man and according to his growth and
standing in grace. Paul was not at all discouraged because Epenetus
was the first fruits of Achaia unto Christ (Rom. 16:5), and
Andronicus and Junia, who were of note among the apostles and
in Christ, were before him (Romans 16:7). If Paul was not
discouraged, why should you be discouraged to see other Christians
outstrip you? It may be that they are of longer standing than you.

2. It may be you judge and compare yourself with others at a great
disadvantage. As first, it may be you compare yourself and your
praying in secret with the praying of others in public. Now this is
very disadvantageous, for in public, men not only have inward but
also outward encouragements, and so through the corruption that
is in all of our hearts, they are more drawn forth at that time than
in secret.

3. It may be you compare their expression with your affection. It may be there is more in your affections than in the multitude of their expressions. You are not to compare your affections with the multitude of other men's words.

4. It may be you compare your prayers with others when they are at their best and highest, and you are at your worst and lowest. There is a great difference between a man and himself during various seasons of life. You judge unequally if you compare yourself in that manner.

In some cases this may be no discouragement to you, such as:

a.) If you are weaker in natural gifts. Though good affections flow from grace, yet good expressions proceed from the goodness of natural abilities as well.

b.) In the case when you have not been a believer for a long period of time.

c.) In the case when you have less time and opportunities for prayer by reason of necessary cares and encumbering employments. When Jonah entered into the ship, there was a great storm. Now all the mariners were at prayer, and every man cried to his god, but Jonah was fast asleep. Now, one would have thought that Jonah had been a most stupid man. But the reason was the greatness of his journey which caused him to be so heavy in sleep. It may be a man that has less grace than you may pray better than you because he is not troubled with these worldly encumbrances that you are necessarily engaged in.

5. God does not distribute gifts and graces to all alike. God has not appointed that all men should grow in grace alike. To this purpose, I may apply a verse from Nehemiah. "Mattaniah, the son of Mica, the son of Zabdi, the son of Asaph was the principal to begin the

thanksgiving in prayer, and Bakbukiah, the second among his brethren, and Abda, the son of Shammua, the third" (Neh. 11:17). God does not intend that all should be alike in grace or gifts. God has his first, second, and third; one may fall short of another, and yet all have truth of grace; yea, all have some growth in grace. Another may pray better, yet you may pray well. Another may pray more affectionately, yet you may pray as acceptably in the sight of God.

Now for the second reason that God's people doubt that they have a holy importunity when they really have it: Many a poor soul may say, "I can remember when I used to pray better and more largely than I do now. If I could pray better before, I must have grown remiss and lack importunity." But this is no sound reason because:

1. It may be that before you had more affection but less judgment, experience, and spirituality in your prayers. But now you have grown in knowledge and inward holiness. You can make more inward prayer to God now because you have more inward communion with God. If this is true, you have no cause to be discouraged. God loves a judicious prayer as well as a large and affectionate prayer. You see what you lack in one way, you make up in another. A young carpenter gives more blows and makes more chips, but an old and experienced workman does the best work. A young musician can play more quickly and nimbly upon an instrument, but an old musician has more skill.

2. It may be when you had more affections in prayer, you also had more sin in prayer, more pride in your gifts, more dependence upon your duties, more censoriousness of others, and many other corruptions that accompanied your prayers and your affections in them. Though you have fewer affections now, yet those other corruptions are in great part eaten out.

3. It may be you do not have as many helps and opportunities to keep up your heart and stir up your affections in prayer as you had formerly. It may be you formerly lived under the teachings of an able godly minister. Now you have lost that opportunity.

4. Though it is true that you are abated and you prayed better before, yet this should not be a matter of discouragement to you if:

a.) It does not proceed from a voluntary carelessness.

b.) It is not accompanied with hardness and insensibleness.

c.) It is not continued in with laziness and contentedness.

The third reason God's people doubt that they have a holy importunity when they truly have it is this: They complain that they do not have those enlarged expressions in prayer which God's people usually have. For an answer, consider these things:

1. It has many times been the case of God's own people that they have lacked expressions, and they could not find a vent for their affections. Thus it was with Hannah. She spoke in her heart, but she was not able to express herself. So it was with David. "I am so troubled that I cannot speak" (Psa. 77:4). Yet in the first verse of that psalm he tells us that he cried unto the Lord with his voice. Here was a heart full of prayer though he lacked utterance.

2. It is better to have affections without expressions than expressions without affections. God looks more to the desires of the heart than the words of the mouth. It may be what you lack in expression is made up in affection.

3. It may be that what is lacking in words is made up in life. As you are defective in expression, so you may make a recompense in your Christian walk, and that is the best expression that can be. It is much better to live a prayer than to express a prayer. It is good to

pray for grace, but it is better to live a life of grace. It is good to pray against sin, but it is better to live against sin.

The fourth ground of doubting a holy importunity is this: Many a disconsolate Christian is apt to say, "I am troubled with wandering thoughts and dullness of heart in prayer." I confess your case is sad and to be lamented, and it is just a matter of humiliation. Yet even here is matter of comfort:

a.) If you do what you can to free yourself from wanderings before you come to pray.

b.) If you do what you can to resist wanderings during prayer.

c.) If you are sensible of these wanderings afterward.

If you can say that you do these three things in an attempt to avoid wanderings, your wanderings shall never be laid to your charge. And thus, I have addressed both of these cautions and the principal doctrine which is this: Holy importunity and earnestness of spirit is a condition required in the prayers of God's people if they expect returns and answers to prayer.

Chapter 8

Evidence of Answered Prayer

ॐ

I say unto you, though he will not rise and give to him because he
is his friend, yet because of his importunity, he will give him as
much as he needs.
Luke 11:8

THERE is another considerable doctrine yet taken from the
amplification of the concession: "He asked only three loaves, yet
because of his importunity, he will give him as much as he needs."

The observation is this: When the heart is importunate in begging
mercy, God usually gives us more then we pray for.

In the handling of this doctrine:

    1. I shall prove it by Scripture-instances.

    2. I shall lay down the reasons of it.

    3. I shall answer some objections and cases of conscience.

First, I shall prove it by Scripture instances. You have the example
of Hannah. She begged for a son with much importunity, being a
woman of a sorrowful spirit for want of a son, and God answered
her. Chemnitius observes, "Hannah asked a son, and God gave her
a prophet. She begged a son, and God gave her a gracious son—a
son greatly beloved of God. She asked a single mercy, and God
gave her a double blessing."

Another instance you have in Abraham (Gen. 17). Abraham prayed, "O that Ishmael might live in your sight." Well, what answer does God return? "Sarah, your wife, shall bear you a son indeed, and you shall call his name Isaac, and I will establish my covenant with him for an everlasting covenant and with his seed after him." It was Abraham's desire that Ishmael might live. Now God not only granted his request but granted him a better mercy.

Another instance you have in the Canaanite woman who importunately begged for the life and health of her daughter (Matt. 15). Christ answered her, "Be it unto you even as you will."

Now, if you ask why God deals this way with his people, I answer:

1. This proceeds from the largeness and greatness of God's power and the riches and freeness of his grace towards us. "Now unto him who is able to do exceeding abundantly above all that we are able to ask or think, according to the power that works in us" (Eph. 3:20). A man may ask of another man, and it may be received, but then he must not ask again. But herein appears the power, ability, goodness, and bounty of God: If we ask of him once or twice, he is a God that is able to give, not according to our asking only, but above what we ask; and not only above what we can ask, but above what we can ask or think. The words are so full that they cannot well be expressed, "God does more than excessively." God has not only a fullness of abundance, but of redundancy; not only of plenty, but bounty. He is better than our prayers.

2. God will do this to relieve his people and to supply their spiritual wants. Among the wants of God's people there is this one: that we do not know what we need nor what we should pray for (Rom. 8:26). Therefore, God supplies our wants not only in what we ask but in what we want though we do not pray for it.

So much for the reasons. I now come to answer some objections.

Objection 1. Some may say, "What privilege has a godly man more than a wicked man, seeing we read of wicked men that prosper in the world and have more than the heart can wish (Psa. 73)?"

Answer 1. It is true that in temporal mercies, God may give wicked men more than the godly and more than their hearts can wish, but God does not give them spiritual mercies, as we may see in Balaam. God gave Balaam honors and riches, but Balaam cried out, "O that I might die the death of the righteous." This God did not grant him. Likewise, many wicked men say in a general way, "Lord pardon my sins," but God does not hear them. It may be that a child of God might ask of God temporal mercies, and God will give him spiritual mercies. This is more than he asked and much better than he gives to wicked men.

Answer 2. Though God gives wicked men more than their hearts can wish, yet God does not give it as a return of prayer, but only as the fruit of common providence, since they are his creatures whom he will preserve.

Answer 3. God may give wicked men more than their hearts can wish, and this is not in mercy but in wrath. They may receive mercies, but not in mercy. There are four demonstrations when God hears a man in wrath.

1.) When he asks anything of God that is sinful in its own nature. As the denial of it is an act of mercy, so the granting of it is a fruit of God's anger. Many times God gives those things in anger which he denies when he is well pleased. God will not hear his own people according to their wills but according to his own will. It is in this case as it is with a father when his child, for want of knowledge, asks him for a knife by which he may cut his fingers. The father will not give him the knife except in wrath. So a man may ask mercies at the hand of God, and it may be God will give them in wrath to cut themselves with them.

2.) If you ask those things of God which are not sinful in their own nature, but if asking of them be to an unlawful end, God will deny these in mercy. If when he gives them, it is in wrath. So it was in Psalm 78:18. They tempted God in their hearts and asked meat for their lust. They desired a lawful thing for unlawful ends. But what followed? The wrath of God. For while the meat was in their mouths, the wrath of God came upon them (verses 30, 31).

3.) If you ask anything of God and he gives it in wrath, you may know by this: if it is an occasion of sin to you, it is given you in wrath. So it was with the Israelites, even now mentioned, the meat that God gave them proved an occasion of sin (verse 32). They sinned still and believed not his wondrous works. When the mercies you enjoy become fuel to your lusts, those mercies are accompanied with the curse and wrath of God. This using of mercies will turn to the aggravation of wrath.

4.) Mercies are given in wrath when the enjoyment of them hinders you from the receipt of greater mercies from God. Thus it was with the devils (Matt. 8:31-32). They begged Christ that they might go into the herd of swine. Christ granted them to enter the swine that they might not enter men. When the giving of temporal mercies hinders you from the receipt of spiritual mercies, they are given in wrath. There are many men to whom God gives temporal mercies. They have riches in abundance, pleasure at will, everything they can desire, but these mercies take their thoughts and affections away from better things. By getting these, they lose Christ, grace, immortality, and eternal happiness. Now in these cases, though God does give temporal mercies, yet they are given in wrath. Notwithstanding this objection, the privilege of God's people is much greater than the privilege of wicked men.

Objection 2. But it may be further objected and enquired, if this is so, that mercies are given to wicked men in wrath and by a common providence, how may I know when mercies come to me as returns of prayers?

Now I shall answer that in these particulars:

Answer 1. Mercies are returns of prayer when the receiving of mercy is a means to quicken the heart to beg for other mercies at the hands of God. When the mercy shall make you love prayer more and use prayer more, it is a return of prayer. This you find proved by David's experience. "Because he has heard my voice, therefore I will call upon him as long as I live" (Psa. 116:2). You see here that because God heard David's prayer and gave him the mercy he begged, he committed to pray as long as he lived. So to continue in prayer is a means to get more mercy. The leaving off of prayer when you have a mercy is a means to lose that which you have obtained at the hands of God. As for the wicked, it is not so with them. Mercies received only from common providence have no such efficacy, as you may see in Job. "The wicked live, become old, yea, mighty in power. Their seed is established in their sight with them, and their offspring before their eyes. Their houses are safe from fear, neither is the rod of God upon them" (Job 21:7-8). And so he goes on, describing that happy condition of wicked men and how God followed them with mercy after mercy. Well, what was the effect of this? Did this engage them to call upon God? Did this make them fall in love with prayer? No, it had a contrary effect (verse 14). They said to God, "Depart from us, for we do not desire the knowledge of your ways. . . .What is the Almighty that we should serve him? And what profit should we have if we pray unto him?"

Answer 2. Mercies that are given as returns of prayer do not only make a man consider that they are from God but draw the heart to God and put a man upon employing them in service to the honor of God. This we find to be the temper of Hannah (I Sam. 1:27-28).

Hannah prayed for a child; God gave her a son. Now, what does she do with this mercy? Observe: "For this child I prayed, and the Lord has granted my petition. Therefore, I have lent him to the Lord as long as he lives." In essence she was saying, "Seeing God has heard my prayer and granted my request, therefore, I will give this mercy back to God to be employed in his service." So also, "And whatsoever we ask, we receive of him because we keep his commandments and do those things that are pleasing in his sight" (I John 3:22). You see, it is made evident that what we receive as an answer to our asking is received because we make those mercies helps to obedience in keeping God's commandments. But mercies that come from a common providence do not draw out the heart toward God. Rather, they draw it out toward sin as it was mentioned in Psalm 78. Though God gave them their hearts' desire, yet they were not estranged from their lusts.

Answer 3. Mercies come from God as returns of prayer when they make you rejoice more in the fact that God hears your prayers than in the mercy you receive from God. For example, Hannah asked for a son, and God gave her a son, yet she said, "My heart rejoices in the Lord" (I Sam. 2:1). God gave her a son. She rejoiced in that mercy, but she rejoiced more in the God who gave it. So it was with David. "Will you not revive us again that your people may rejoice in you?" (Psa. 85:6). We will not rejoice chiefly in the mercy but in you, O Lord. On the contrary, those who receive mercies out of the basket of common providence rejoice more in the mercy than in the God of mercy. They rejoice in their wealth and glory, in the multitude of their riches. But as for God, they bid him to depart from them. They cannot rejoice in God.

Answer 4. Mercies that are the fruit of prayer are known by this: He that has them ascribes them not to his own industry but to the grace of God. For example, when Samson was ready to die for thirst, he prayed unto the Lord, and God clave a hollow place in the jaw-bone and gave him water. Now Samson called the name of the place Enhakkore, "The well of him that prayed." He ascribed it to the return of his prayers, to that assistance that God gave him to pray. So Hannah ascribed her mercy to God, not herself. But a wicked man that receives mercies from God's general providence, his language is, "This I have labored for. This I have ventured my life for. This I got by my forecast, effort, and industry." They sacrifice to their own nets but seldom say, "This is the return of prayers—this is the gift of God."

Answer 5. The mercy that is given as a return of prayer is enjoyed with more quiet and contentment of mind than when it is given by general providence. When Eli told Hannah that she should have a son, she had so much inward joy and contentment of mind that it is said, "Hannah went away rejoicing, and her countenance was no longer sad." The consideration of that made her rejoice. The reason is because mercies that are given as returns of prayer are given with a blessing and inward quietness of mind. The mercies that God gives his people are given with joy and comfort. "The blessing of the Lord makes rich, and he adds no sorrow to it" (Prov. 10:22). You read in I Chron. 4:10, "And Jabez called on the God of Israel, saying, 'O that you would bless me indeed, and enlarge my coasts, and that your hand might be with me, and that you would keep me from evil that it may not grieve me.' " Jabez knew that it was the manner of God when he gave blessings as returns of prayer not to add grief to it. Isaac prayed for a wife, and God gave her to be a great comfort to him. It may be wicked men have wives and no contentment with them but sorrow added to them because they did not pray for them as Isaac did. They have children but sorrow with them, and they have abundance of riches but sorrow added with it all because they do not have the mercies as returns of prayer. The mercies that are given in a way of general providence are usually accompanied with vexation and discontent, snares and sorrows. "He gave them their requests, but he sent leanness into their souls" (Psa. 106:15). God gives wicked men their requests, but is it with a blessing and with content? No, they have it with a curse. You know Saul gave Michal to David to be a snare to him, a cross, and discontentment. So many times, in just judgment, God gives his blessings to wicked men to be snares, curses, and crosses to them.

Answer 6. Mercies that come as returns of prayer may be known by this: if they are given in the time when God draws out your heart to seek him in holy duties. An instance of this you have in Acts. While the church met to pray for Peter's enlargement, the prison-doors were opened. Peter came and knocked at the door of the house where they were assembled. This was an evident sign that God gave them as a return of prayer. "When they had prayed, the place was shaken where they were assembled together; and they were all filled with the Holy Spirit" (Acts 4:31). You read in John 4:52-53 that the noble man enquired diligently concerning the time wherein the child began to recover. When he was told, he knew it was the return of his prayer and a fruit of Christ's love. God tells his people, "Before they call, I will answer, and while they are yet speaking, I will hear" (Isa. 65:24). Thus, we read in the Book of Martyrs, "That the people of God did make it a sign of God's answering prayers when God was pleased to give mercies at the time wherein they prayed." Thus, we read of Luther, "That there was a young man who had made a covenant and sealed a bond with his own blood to give himself, soul and body, to the devil, only to live in pleasure and have whatsoever he desired. When the time of the bond was almost out, he being much troubled in his mind, came to Luther and told him what he had done and what was likely to befall him upon it. Whereupon Luther called the church together and kept a solemn fast on behalf of the young man. And while Luther was in prayer, being earnest with God, there was a great noise heard amongst them, and the bond was cast into the lap of Luther in the midst of the congregation. So for time to come, the young man led a holy and godly life."

Answer 7. Lastly, mercies are given as answers to prayer when you commit to fulfill those vows which you made to God before you enjoyed the mercy. But when we promise God largely before we have the mercy, and when we receive the mercy but do not perform the vows, it is an argument that we have the mercy by general and common providence. "You shall make your prayer unto him, and he shall hear you. You shall pay your vows. You shall also decree a thing, and it shall be established unto you, and the light shall shine upon your ways" (Job 22:27-28). So when you beg a mercy and say, 'Lord, give me such a mercy, and I will do thus and thus. I will walk so and so before you. I will improve them to your glory,' God will hear. But then you must be sure to perform your vows. This frame of heart we find in David. "I will go into your house with burnt offerings. I will pay my vows which my lips have uttered and my mouth has spoken when I was in trouble" (Psa. 66:13-14). David was in trouble, and he prayed to God and made vows in case God would deliver him. Now God did deliver him out of trouble, and he made good on his vows. Here was a return of prayer. David did not grow secure and careless, but he made conscience to pay what he had promised God. So you see how you may discover whether the mercies you receive from God are returns of prayer or only fruits of common providence.

Objection 3. Another objection or case of conscience is this: How can it be true that God gives his people more than they need, seeing it is the complaint of God's people many times that they have been a long time begging mercy. Many say, "I pray for pardon of sin, and I cannot get it pardoned. I pray daily for power against my corruptions, and yet I cannot get my lusts subdued? What then shall I think of my prayers?"

Now to this I shall lay down several things by way of answer.

Answer 1. It must be considered that God gets glory by the denials of his people. And if the denying of a mercy to you be the way of advice, it is better that God should have his glory and you be without the mercy than that you should have the mercy and God lack his glory. An eminent instance you have in John 12. There was a prayer made by Mary and Martha for their brother Lazarus. "And they came unto Jesus and said, 'He whom you love is sick.' But Jesus said, 'This sickness is not unto death, but for the glory of God.' " When Jesus heard that he was sick, he stayed two days in the place where he was, though he loved Martha, and he loved Lazarus, yet he stayed two days and would not go to him. But in verse 14 Christ said plainly, " 'Lazarus is dead. And I am glad for your sakes that I was not there to the intent that you might believe.' But they said unto him, 'Lord, if you had been here, he would not have died.' " Christ came and commanded them to roll the stone away. Martha answered, "He has been four days in the grave, and by this time he stinks." This was what Christ aimed at: He knew that it was greater glory for him to raise the dead out of the grave than to raise him out of the bed of sickness. The power of the Godhead appeared more in the former than in the latter. And when Martha told him, "He stinks," Jesus answered, "Did I not say unto you that if you believed you would see the glory of God?" That is, you should see the power of my Godhead. This was the end of Christ's denying of mercy, though it was earnestly desired, yet a greater mercy was given for his greater glory.

Answer 2. It may be you do not hear God in his commands, so then it is no wonder God does not hear your prayers. If you do not hearken to the call of God, it may be expected that God will not hearken to your call. "Because I have called, and you refused. I have stretched out my hand, and no man regarded" (Prov. 1:24). "Then shall they call upon me, but I will not answer; they shall seek me early, but they shall not find me" (Prov. 1:28). "Then they shall cry unto the Lord, but he will not hear them; he will even hide his face from them at that time, as they have behaved themselves ill in their doings" (Mic. 3:4). "'Therefore, it is come to pass that as he cried and they would not hear, so they cried, and I would not hear,' says the Lord of Hosts" (Zech. 7:13). It may be God has been calling you to repent and believe for many years—to be reformed, to forsake the evil of your doings, yet you have not heeded his call. His mercies have not drawn you. His judgments have not affrighted you. Is it not just with God to let you call and he not hear you?

Answer 3. It may be you ask but slightly, and therefore your prayers are not successful. As it is with a man who asks anything of another man slightly and coldly, he does, as it were, desire him to say him no. So when a man asks mercies of God carelessly and indifferently, this provokes God to give no answer. It may be that your prayers are sleepy and drowsy with a wandering heart. And do you think God will hear that prayer that you do not hear yourself? Do you think that God will accept that prayer when you know not what you say?

Answer 4. God may give you a mercy, and you, through your unbelief, impatience, and inobservance, do not acknowledge the return or answer God gives. God may hear your prayers, yet you take no notice of it. This you see in Job. "If I have called and God answered, yet I will not believe that God has heard me because you break me with your tempest" (Job 9:16-17). Job was in a fit of impatience and unbelief, and though God did give him return of prayer, he did not observe it.

Answer 5. God may deny you the mercy, not that he is unable or unwilling to hear you, but to make you more desirous of and so more fit for mercy. It may be you are not fit for an answer. The philosopher begged money of Antigonus. He gave him a drachme.

He said, "It is not for a king to give so little; a talent had been a more suitable gift." The king replied, "Though a talent is fit for me to give, yet you are not fit to receive." So, though God is always fit and ready to give an answer to our prayers, yet we are not always fit and ready to receive the answer. God bids us open our mouths wide, "and I will fill it." God denies us that we may open our mouths the wider and enlarge our desires the more after mercy. The Lord is toward his people like a father to his child. A father may seem to withdraw and hide himself from his child to test its love to him. The child begins to mourn and cry, yet the father does not come to the child. But when he hears the child cry aloud, then he comes to it and takes it up in his arms. So many times the Lord sees his people pray and seems to withdraw from them, to hide from the prayers of his people. He goes, as it were, out of their sight until they begin to cry aloud and be very earnest and importunate in their prayers, till their desires are enlarged towards God. Then God graciously returns their prayers into their bosom. Now this is a very good reason why God denies the prayers of his people. Desires deferred grow stronger, but if the mercies are soon given, the desires grow cold and the mercy grows contemptible. Manna comes quickly and is lightly regarded. God does with us as a fisherman— he draws back the bait that the fish may come after it more eagerly and bite harder. God seems to draw back a mercy that we may more earnestly pursue it.

Answer 6. Consider that God's people have prayed and waited a long time before God has given them an answer to their prayers. God promised Abraham that a son should proceed from him in whom all the families of the earth should be blessed and that his seed should be multiplied as the stars in the firmament. Yet it was fifteen years between the time of God's promise and the accomplishment of it. Likewise, you find it with Zachariah and Elizabeth. They prayed for a child at the beginning of their marriage. Now God heard their cries and prayers, but he did not give them a return till they were old and stricken in years. So it was with the church. "When I cry and shout, he shuts out my prayer" (Lam. 3:8). "You have covered yourself with a cloud that our prayers should not pass through" (Lam. 3:44). So also it was in Habakkuk. "O Lord, how long shall I cry, and you will not hear?" (Hab. 1:2). It was also the complaint of David. "My God, my God, why have you forsaken me? Why are you so far from helping me and from the words of my roaring? O my God, I cry in the daytime and you hear not, and in the night season, and I am not silent" (Psa. 22:1-2).

Answer 7. God may not only defer or deny to hear his people's prayers, but in some times and cases, he is angry with the prayers of his people. "O Lord God of hosts, how long will you be angry with the prayers of your people" (Psa. 80:4). "I cry unto you, and you do not hear me. I stand up and you regard me not; you are cruel to me with your strong hand; you oppose yourself against me" (Job 30:20-21).

Answer 8. Consider this for your comfort: Your person may be accepted and your prayers may be heard, yet the thing you pray for may not be granted. An instance of this you have in Christ himself. He prayed, "Father, if it is possible, let this cup pass from me" (Matt. 26:39). But the cup did not pass from him. He drank of it, yet it is said that Christ was heard in all that he prayed (Heb. 5:7). Another example is Moses. "I sought the Lord at that time . . . but the Lord was wroth with me for your sakes and would not hear me. And the Lord said unto me, 'Let it suffice you, speak no more to me of this matter' " (Deut. 3:23-26). Moses importunately desired that he might see the promise land and go over the Jordan to possess it. Moses was a godly man, and here he prayed for this mercy. But God was angry with him and commanded him to pray no more. God told him to go up the mount to see the land but that he should not go into it. So when you ask a particular mercy at the hand of God, God may deny that mercy and yet hear your prayers and accept your person.

Answer 9. God may deny the mercy you ask and give you a better one in place of it. He makes you open your mouth the wider that he might give you the greater mercies. Abraham prayed that Ishmael might live. Now God did not hear his prayer, as Abraham desired it, but he gave him Isaac, and with him, he established the covenant, which was a better mercy. Moses was denied his request to go into Canaan, but he was translated into a better place, into the true Canaan.

Answer 10. God may deny what we pray for in mercy because if he were to grant it, it would be a token of his wrath. As if a man should ask that which was sinful, or that which would be an unavoidable occasion of sin, or if he should ask it for sinful ends, or it would be a monument of his shame. All which cases I have spoken to before and therefore shall now say no more.

Answer 11. God may hear another man's prayers for you though he will not hear your own. This is a great comfort to every poor weak Christian in the world—they have a stock of prayers going for them to the throne of grace. You read in Job that God forbade his three friends to pray but told Job to pray for them, assuring Job that he would hear him for them. "Go to my servant Job and offer up for yourselves a burnt offering, and my servant Job shall pray for you; for him will I accept, lest I deal with you after your folly, in that you have not spoken of me the thing that is right like my servant Job" (Job 42:8-9). They did as God commanded them, and the Lord accepted Job. It may be there are times when you cannot pray, or when God will not hear your prayers, but remember you have a stock of prayers going for you. I now come to make application.

Chapter 9

Encouragements and Cautions

❧

I say unto you, though he will not rise and give to him because he
is his friend, yet because of his importunity, he will give him as
much as he needs.

Luke 11:8

IN the first place, let me draw some inferences or corollaries from
what has been insisted upon.

Corollary 1. Returns or answers to prayer are not given for the
work's sake but for the person's sake. Though the matter of your
prayer may be good, yet if you are not a good man, you shall not be
accepted. God first had respect to Abel and then to his offering.
"The righteous cry, and the Lord hears" (Psa. 34:17). The person
must be in a state of favor before the duty can be accepted.

Corollary 2. Though prayers are not returned for the work, yet they
are not returned without the work. God expects the work, and you
must do good works, though God will not have you look for
acceptance for the work's sake.

Corollary 3. The return of prayers is not made to a person singularly
considered but as to a member of Christ, as one that has a share in
his intercession. "If you abide in me, you shall ask what you will,
and it shall be given you" (Jn. 15:7). "Whatever you ask of the
Father in my name, that he will give you" (Jn. 16:23). All our prayers
are but ciphers till Christ's intercession be added. Ciphers in
arithmetic stand for nothing till a figure is added.

Corollary 4. The longer and more often you have prayed, the more affectionate you should be in prayer. "Ask and you shall have, seek and you shall find, knock and it shall be opened unto you" (Matt. 6:7). Observe the gradation in these words: Ask, but you must not stay there—you must seek. Nor can you rest satisfied there—you must knock. Your affections should be every day more eager and earnest. You should pray more fervently as it is said of Christ (Luke 22:44).

Corollary 5. He can never pray importunately who does not pray daily. Intermission of duty will quickly cause an interruption in your affections. You must pray in secret, pray fervently, pray morning and evening. To stir you up and encourage you in this work:

Consider 1. Consider the example of those holy men of God who have done this. "Let your ear now be attentive and open that you may hear the prayer of your servant which I pray before you day and night" (Neh. 1:6). So you have the example of Daniel. "He kneeled upon his knees three times a day and prayed and gave thanks before his God, as he did before time" (Dan. 6:10). It was a custom that he had observed in former times. Though he was a great courtier and a man full of great employment, yet he would not neglect prayer. Nor was this an extraordinary fit but his ordinary course. So in David, "My voice you shall hear in the morning, and in the evening I will direct my prayer unto you and will look up" (Psa. 5:3). "But unto you have I cried, O Lord, and in the morning shall my prayer come to you" (Psa. 88:13). "I rose before the dawn and cried unto the Lord" (Psa. 119:147). "Evening and morning and at noon I will pray and cry aloud" (Psa. 55:17).

Consider 2. You have the example of Jesus Christ himself. "In the morning, rising up a great while before day, he went out and departed into a solitary place, and there prayed, and so at evening" (Mark 1:35). "He went to a mountain to pray, and when the evening had come, he was there also" (Matt. 14:23). And lest you should think this was only upon an extraordinary occasion, "He came to the Mount of Olives *as was his custom*" (Luke 22:3). "Jesus had *often* met there with his disciples" (John 18:2).

Consider 3. You have the very examples of heathens in this. The heathens sacrificed to Hercules morning and evening upon the great altar at Rome.

Consider 4. In the Lord's Prayer, we are taught to pray every day. Christ did not tell us to pray for bread or what we need for a month or a year, but to pray day by day.

Consider 5. This was prefigured in the Law. There was a daily offering to be given to God—a lamb at morning and a lamb at night (Ex. 29:38-39). Extraordinary sacrifices did not abolish this number. There was a burnt offering and an offering for the Sabbath, besides the continual offering, the burnt offering at the beginning of the month and the Passover offering; and though these extraordinary works were to be done, yet the ordinary works were not to be left undone. Here is good ground and encouragement to be frequent in these religious duties.

This may be useful for the instruction of those to whom God has given returns of prayer and to whom God has given out of his bounty more than they asked. To such, I must first give some negative cautions and then some positive cautions.

Negative Caution 1. Do not let God's answers to your prayers make you remiss and careless in prayer. Beware of an empty heart when God brings in your mercies with a full hand. If merchant adventurers have good returns, they are encouraged to adventure their ships to sea again. Our hearts are so base and disingenuous that when we have what we seek for, we are apt to seek no more. Beware not to let God's goodness make you worse.

Negative Caution 2. Do not let returns or answers to prayer make you conceited and proud of your gifts or graces. We are too apt to reflect upon ourselves, our graces, our abilities. Beware that your heart is not lifted up in pride against God, lest God be provoked to lift up his hand against you in judgment.

Negative Caution 3. Beware that you do not ascribe the answers or returns of prayer to your own importunity but to the freeness of God's grace. God cannot endure to give his glory to another. Rather say, "I have received mercy, but alas, there is nothing in me that could deserve it. All comes solely from the free grace of God."

Negative Caution 4. Beware of returning again to sin after God has returned your prayers into your bosom with gracious answers. "I will hear what the Lord God will speak, for he will speak peace to his people, but let them not turn again to folly" (Psa. 85:8). It would be both sin and folly to return to sin after God has given you an answer of peace. This was David's resolution for his own particular situation. "Depart from me all you workers of iniquity" (Psa. 6:8). What is the reason? "The Lord has heard the voice of my supplication." As if David had said, "O you wicked men, you have been occasions of sin to me and companions in sin with me, but now that God has graciously returned my prayers, I will have no more to do with you. Depart from me, you workers of iniquity." And so much for the negative cautions. I shall now lay down a few positive cautions.

Positive Caution 1. If God has returned your prayers, see that you are more frequent in prayer than you were formerly. This was the purpose of David. "Because the Lord has heard my prayer, therefore I will call upon him as long as I live" (Psa. 116:2). So let it be your care to set yourself more solemnly and seriously to seek God than you have ever done before.

Positive Caution 2. See that you praise God more than you ever have before. Those mercies that you have won by prayer are to be worn with thankfulness. "All your works praise you, O Lord, and your saints do bless you" (Psa. 145:10). All God's works praise him. The heavens declare the glory of God, and the firmament shows his handy work. That is, they are all the passive monuments of God's power in creating them. But the saints are active agents in praising God. Their mouths are full of the praises of God. They have a principle within them of praising God. They are agents in setting forth his praise. Therefore, it is very fit that you should bless God.

Positive Caution 3. See that you be much in obedience to God. If God does much for you, see that you do much for Him. If God has a hearing ear, you must have a doing hand. And so much for the use of caution.

I shall now speak something by way of comfort to:

1. Such as have not this importunity nor this return of prayers.

2. Such as have returns of prayer.

Here is a word of consolation to those that want this holy importunity yet do not have it; and that in three respects.

Consolation 1. You may pray with sincerity when you do not pray with importunity. "The Lord," says David, "is near to all that call upon him." But how? Not only to them that call on him importunately and powerfully but to all that call upon him in truth. If you can say that you call upon God in truth and with a sincere heart, God will be near to you.

Consolation 2. It is the office of Christ to pray for you in heaven when you do not pray upon earth. It is the work of Jesus Christ to make intercession for you to his Father. Although you do not have

79

importunity in yourself, yet consider, O believing soul, that Christ is in heaven importuning the Father for you.

Consolation 3. A sense and complaining of the lack of this holy importunity is accounted by God to actually be a degree of importunity. If you never complained of the lack of the Spirit, it would be a sign you never had the Spirit. Now that you grieve your lack of importunity, it is a sign that you have it.

Here are words of encouragement to those that have returns of prayer:

Encouragement 1. Your mercies are double mercies. It is a mercy to have mercy, but to have it as a return of prayer is a double mercy. "They shall call upon me, and I will answer them, and I will be with him in trouble" (Psa. 91:15). It is a mercy to have deliverance out of trouble, but to have it through prayer, a deliverance that comes in by prayer, that is a double mercy indeed.

Encouragement 2. These mercies are sanctified mercies. Mercies are good, but mercies that are returns of prayer are sanctified. And blessed mercies are much better to the soul that enjoys them.

Encouragement 3. The mercies which you have as returns of prayer are costly mercies. Mercies that come in by providence are easy and cheap, but mercies that come in by prayer are costly. They cost the price of Christ's blood to purchase them, and they cost you many a prayer and tear to obtain them.

Encouragement 4. These mercies are sealing mercies, and that in three particulars:

a.) They are seals to you that you have the Spirit of God, for Christ hears no prayers and no spirit but his own. God is as well pleased with the barking of a dog as with the prayers of a Christ-less man.

b.) It is a seal to you of an interest in Christ's intercession. If your prayers are returned, it is a sign they are accepted. Now, no prayers are accepted but by virtue of the intercession of Jesus Christ.

c.) These returns are a seal of more mercies—a sign that you shall have more mercies from God. One mercy that is given by prayer is a pledge of another mercy. Your mercies in this life are a pledge to you that you shall have eternal happiness in heaven to all eternity.

FINIS

Made in United States
Cleveland, OH
18 June 2025

17808016R00046